The Bronx Years

poems by

Christine Baldino O'Hanlon

Finishing Line Press
Georgetown, Kentucky

The Bronx Years

Copyright © 2023 by Christine Baldino O'Hanlon
ISBN 979-8-88838-149-6 First Edition
All rights reserved under International and Pan-American Copyright Conventions.
No part of this book may be reproduced in any manner whatsoever without written
permission from the publisher, except in the case of brief quotations embodied in
critical articles and reviews.

Publisher: Leah Huete de Maines
Editor: Christen Kincaid
Cover Art: Erv Dea-Jue
Author Photo: Brian O'Hanlon
Cover Design: Elizabeth Maines McCleavy

Order online: www.finishinglinepress.com
also available on amazon.com

Author inquiries and mail orders:
Finishing Line Press
P. O. Box 1626
Georgetown, Kentucky 40324
U. S. A.

Table of Contents

Italy

The Italian Cavalry Officer 1
The Cavalry Officer's Fiancée 2

America

A Tale of Two Families 5
Grandma Sara tells me she fell in love with the butcher 6
Grandma Teresa warns me not to marry too young 7
My Father's War 8
The Wedding I Didn't Attend 9
Teresa, 30 years later 10
My paternal grandparents 11
Grandpa B. means well 12

The Bronx Years

The truth about skating 15
Parkchester, SE Bronx, 1950s 16
My cousin, my big sister, Joyce 17
Sundays at Grandma and Grandpa C's house 18
Beach Saturdays 19
Trick-or-Treating, Interrupted, 1957 20
Christmas Lights 21
Escape from my sickbed 22
The gift 23
Going fishing with Grandpa C. 24
Our lady 25
My Dad and the nun 26
Pride 27

II

Not a fairy tale 31
St. Raymond's Academy for Girls 32
Walks around the block with Grandpa C. 33
Fruit 34
Squirrels vs. fruit trees 35
Dandelion wine 36
Aunts 37
Uncles 38
Playing with sharks 39
The disastrous date at the Bronx Zoo 40

III

Love and Politics 43
Thomas More College, Fordham University 44
My dad and the Vietnam War 45
First dance 46
Our story 47
Being in love in the Bronx Botanical Gardens 48
Advice 49
You're invited to celebrate 50
Before the South Bronx burned 51

IV

Escape from my Bronx 55
The Godfather Mystique 56
Lust 57
Peace-keeping 58
The Difficulty of Being Your Daughter 59
Baking with Mom 60
Matrilinear 61
Campania on my mind 62
Epilogue 63
Acknowledgments 65

Special thanks

To Nathalie Handal, wondrous poet and teacher. For creating a safe place in your class. For believing I had something to say and could write a collection.

To my writing cohort: Lyn Li Che, Emily Hillebrand, Fatima Malik, Vaughan Meyer and Tracy Tong.

To Matthew Lippman, for your careful and enthusiastic reading of the collection. For your invaluable suggestions.

To Erv Dea-Jue, for the perfect cover photo.

Boundless thanks

To Brian, who's always believed in me.

To Emmet and Courtney, who cheer me on.

To friends who encourage me: Dorothy, Terry, Nancy, Ann, Bill, Miriam, Joe, Alice, John, Judith, Emma and Jo.

Italy

The Italian Cavalry Officer, 1880

Guiseppe Baldino

Everything I know about my great-grandfather
is in a studio photo I have of him.
20 years after the unification of Italy,
Guiseppe Baldino is a serious young man
blessed with a steady job
and a beautiful dark-haired fiancée.
With his short hair, trim mustache and slim build,
my great-grandfather looks handsome in his dress uniform
and shiny riding boots.
In the photo, he's looking off into the future.
In Cosenza, the capital of Calabria,
an agricultural region at the toe of Italy's boot,
many people are either un- or under-employed.
Keeping his job will mean the health and
future of his family.
He'll marry and have one beloved son
before a riding accident kills him.

The Calvary Officer's Fiancée

Giulia Giordano

"I don't know how to say this without seeming vain:
I've always known that I was beautiful.
Since a little girl, men have looked at me
hungrily.
I've received a number of marriage proposals.
I would have liked to have chosen Raffaello,
who makes me laugh.
But he's just an olive grower.
Or Vincenzo with his smoldering good looks.
But my mother thinks Guiseppe will make a better husband.
I saw a radiant smile when I told him 'yes'.
Then he asked if he could kiss me.
I let him.
Now I look forward to the wedding."

America

A tale of two families

During the great migration of Italians to America,
beginning in 1880, two married couples leave Italy.
The Puccis from Calabria are fleeing rural poverty.
The De Grazias from Naples want a fresh start as shopkeepers.
Both settle in New York, around East 116th Street.
They live on different blocks.
In different worlds.

Roughly a decade later, two teenage boys leave Italy,
both named Giuseppe, both orphans.
One from Calabria. The other from Naples.
But the one from Naples has an older brother and
married sister waiting in New York.

Time passes. The Puccis, who don't know any better,
marry off their daughter at 15 to the poor boy from Calabria.
The DeGrazias, more American, let their daughter
choose her husband, the boy from Naples who's
learned a trade.

If we were still in Italy, these families might never meet.
But it's America, where their college-educated children
fall in love and want to marry.
And it's the middle of World War II.

Grandma Sara tells me
she fell in love with the butcher

Sara DeGrazia

"I have to thank Papa for so many things
but particularly for the job he gave me
to buy fresh cold cuts every day for his saloon.

I had an excuse to see Joseph,
the new butcher. He worked for his uncle.
He was nice-looking and had a warmth and
intelligence that reminded me of Papa.

One day, I got quite a shock.
I was out walking with my sister, Nettie, when we both spotted
Joseph's picture in the window of the photographer's shop.
It was still the Italian-American custom to have your picture taken
for your fiancée.

'Oh, no,' said Nettie, voicing my concern. 'You don't think…'
It was only then that I realized how much I cared.

We walked slowly to the butcher's shop.
'Buongiorno,' I tried to say cheerfully, 'my sister and I
saw your photo in the photographer's store window.
Was that taken for your fiancée?'

'No,' he answered, smiling. 'I went to the studio with my friend
who's getting married. The photographer asked
if he could take my picture, too.'

So after that, your grandfather knew how I felt."

Grandma Teresa warns me not to marry too young

Teresa Pucci

"I went from playing with dolls
with my girlfriends to
being betrothed.
I was 15.
I wasn't ready.
My parents picked out the groom,
from Calabria like them.
He was a laborer.
Before I knew it,
I was married and
pregnant with twins.

16

No one told me
what the childbirth would be like:
first the boy, then the girl.
Afterwards, when I was half-dead,
my mother gave me the babies.
Look, Teresa, aren't they beautiful?
I thought 'what a cruel joke.'

17

After my daughter died
I told my husband:
No more children.
I said the doctor advised it.
Joe didn't believe me.
I didn't care.
I lived now for my son, Giovanni."

My father's war

John Baldino

In late 1943, after the worst fighting,
my Dad's Army unit landed in Calabria,
birthplace of his parents.
His grandmother was still living there.

Fluent in Italian, he was liaison to a low-security
prison camp of middle-aged Italian men,
mostly teachers, lawyers, farmers.
They joked with him about the bad American food.

The country seemed in ruins—first the Germans,
then the Brits, now the friendlier Americans.
Dad's fellow G.I.s wanted his help talking to the kids
and the older people running small cantinas.

Before shipping home to work with the wounded,
my father traded favors and loaded a truck full of food.
He drove it up the mountain to meet his grandmother.

The Wedding I Didn't Attend

May 6, 1944

Mom and Dad got engaged by proxy
in the middle of World War II.
Dad, in the Army, in North Africa
asked his parents to choose a ring and
deliver it to Mom.

A year after the engagement, Dad learned
he'd ship home to work with wounded GIs.
He'd have a week's leave.
He asked Mom to plan a wedding.

My parents look radiant in their wedding photo:
Dad in his dress uniform, Mom glowing in her satin gown.
But in the group photo, my grandfathers look worried.
Dad's mother had refused to come to the wedding.
She felt, at 28 years old, Dad was too young to marry.
But he didn't feel young.
He felt grateful to be alive.

Teresa, almost 30 years later

Teresa Pucci Baldino

"My boy Johnny came home from the War
and right away, he had to get married.
He's too young! He's only 28!
I didn't go to the wedding.
Now, before he goes to Atlantic City
to work in the Army hospital,
they are staying with us.
I heard them in the bedroom above,
the laughter, the bed squeaking.
Then she came downstairs to use
the bathroom.
I went into the kitchen and
got a big knife.
When she came out, I surprised her.
I threatened her and screamed curses:
Puttana! Mangia merda e muori!
Now they are leaving to
stay with her family.
Johnny and Joe are angry with me."

My paternal grandparents

Teresa and Joseph Baldino

Their house was tiny.
And they were petite.
As a child, I wondered if they had shrunk.
You entered the house through the basement
to keep the living room clean.
It was like a museum.
Dark walls, covered with large, framed sepia photos.
Heavy dark wooden furniture.

I tried to stay outside.
My father had planted a small garden
behind the house with a shrine to the Virgin Mary.
When we visited, they served one of two things:
Pepsi if we were outside. Liqueurs if we were indoors.
The latter led to my lifelong abstinence
from all aperitifs.

Grandpa B. means well

He didn't know
how to talk to children
so he told the same stories
over and over:
About his father, the cavalry officer, who died so young.
About his mother, the beauty of Cosenza.
About his stepfather who hated him.

The only happiness in his life was
singing in the choir.
He taught me basic Italian:
Come sta?
Uno, due, tre.
Come ti chiami?
But the best thing he taught me,
was the meaning of my name:

Baldino translated *little bold one.*

The Bronx Years

The truth about skating

I got my first pair of roller skates
metal ones that gripped the sides of my shoes
state-of-the-art 1956.
I had a skate key
to adjust the width and length and
leather straps that went around my ankles.

       I took off

We lived in a neighborhood with
lots of asphalt
smooth sailing for me
careening down hills   around curves.
Stopping was harder
than starting.

Sometimes I forgot
I was wearing skates.
One day I wore them
climbing a metal staircase
inside an apartment
building.

I disturbed an old biddy
who reported me to the
neighborhood rent-a-cops.
When they caught up with me,
I gave them a fake name
and address.

       And skated free

Parkchester, SE Bronx
1950s

The place where I grew up
was beautiful with children.

Apartment building after
playground after ball field
packed with noisy
post-war boomers.

I was an only child.
Friends were family.
Pouring out of buildings
on our way to school.
Calling for each other
Hey, wait up!
to go roller-skating or
play racquet ball.

By middle school,
my house was hub
for weekend parties,
thanks to my records—
Fats, Elvis, Chuck Berry—
and no siblings
to heckle
my dance-happy girlfriends.

My cousin, my big sister, Joyce

We didn't feel like only children
we had each other.
Six years between us
it hardly mattered.
Both athletic, we were always outdoors
shooting hoops, playing stoop ball,
riding and diving into waves at Jones Beach.

You led the way into teenage years.
I met all your boyfriends.
I even gave you my opinions.
Then you fell in love
on my 16th birthday.

When I finally met the right guy,
I called you.
I have someone I'd like you to meet.
I could hear your smile over the phone.
What's his name? is what you asked first.

Sundays at Grandma and Grandpa's house

Sara and Joseph Citarella

After Mass, we'd head over to my grandparents' house
in the leafy Pelham part of the North Bronx.
The house was beautiful red brick—my grandfather
had built it for six children who'd outgrown an apartment.

I had three girl cousins. I was the youngest.
I'd see them almost every week so we were like siblings.
I was close to Sara, just two years older.
Closer still to Joyce, an only child, too.

In the winter, while the men played *briscola*
and the women, led by Grandma, played canasta,
we kids loved board games—*Careers, Risk, Monopoly*.
We'd listen to Elvis, Chubby Checkers, Frankie Valli.
I learned to dance.

My oldest cousin tried to boss us around. I ignored her.
In a home video, my dad took of my 1st birthday,
she fusses over my clothes. Without hesitation,
my chubby baby arm firmly swats her out of frame.

Beach Saturdays

Every summer Saturday
late June through Labor Day,
we'd head out to Jones Beach
on the south shore of Long Island.
The Park was created in the 1920s,
six miles of silver-white sand
and Art Deco bath houses.

We'd leave early, around 8 am,
to avoid traffic
which was bumper-to-bumper
on a beautiful summer Saturday.

My Dad was a strong swimmer.
He taught Joyce and me how to dive
into the base of big waves.
It was thrilling—as good as an amusement ride.
Sometimes a wave would surprise us,
knock us underwater, drive us
into the shore.

Did you swallow half the ocean?
my Mom would ask if I ended up at her feet.
She and Aunt Ruth would be standing there,
in their smart sunglasses and beach hats.

Years later, we took our small son to Jones Beach.
We wondered would he run away
or toward the water.
He headed straight into the foam.
And Joyce was waiting to catch him,
my little flying fish.

Trick-or-Treating, **Interrupted**
1957

I'm 7, my cousin Joyce is 13.

We want to go *trick-or-treating*
in her neighborhood,
just to families we know.

For our parents,
it's out of the question.

Uncle Lou comes up
with a compromise.
He dresses up as a hobo
to pass himself off as a kid.

Out we go into the dark October
evening. We had barely started—
two houses, two *Milky Ways*, two apples.

At the 3rd house,
the neighbors turn on the porch light.
At the same moment,
we're joined by a bunch of boys
who know Joyce from school.
*You and your friends want to come
trick-or-treating with us?*
Thanks anyway, Joyce answers quickly.
We have to get home for dinner.

Then one of boys sees something in the light.
Look at that kid's hairy hand!
My uncle hides it quickly in his pocket.
And just as fast, we scamper home
in the darkness.

Christmas Lights

When I was growing up in Parkchester,
a sprawling middle-class apartment complex,
there was always a big Christmas tree display
in its center—at Metropolitan Oval.
The huge pool was emptied, the spouting statues
turned off, and in their place
were dozens of Christmas trees,
decorated with bright balls and
sparkling lights.

A mile away was Morris Park,
a working-class Italian-American enclave
with small houses and front yards.
Their Christmas displays were flashier.

Let's go look at the pizzeria Christmas lights,
my Dad would joke. And we'd take a ride.
Down the block we'd drive slowly,
admiring a nativity scene with shepherds
in one yard,
a big Santa and reindeer on the roof
next door.
Some yards had both—baby Jesus and Santa
sharing the lights.

It was fun. Overdone.
Our Christmas tradition.

Escape from my sickbed

Growing up in the 1950s,
in classrooms of 40-plus students,
I picked up most childhood diseases:
mumps, chicken pox, measles.
Measles was the worst:
I was sick, feverish and forbidden to read.
Something to do with injuring my eyes.
So Mom read to me.
Seated in the big chintz-covered chair by the window
in the corner of my room,
she read *Great Expectations.*
While I, propped up on pillows, under the covers,
joined Pip in the cemetery, helping the convict.

Gift

Grandpa took me to Woolworth's in Ft. Lauderdale.
He pointed to a pile of stuffed Easter toys—
ducks, bunnies, fleecy lambs—
and said, *Pick any one.*
I was 7.

His gift was my power to choose.
I chose a bunny the color of the sea.

Going fishing with Grandpa C.

Every winter I'd look forward
to early summer
when I would be free
from boring school
and could be outdoors
fishing with Grandpa.

We went to City Island
and fished off the pier
or to Robert Moses Park
and surf-cast in the ocean.

Grandpa was the perfect companion
for a ten-year old city girl
who preferred not
to put live worms on a hook
or clobber fish when we caught them.

It was the companionable quiet
and peacefulness
generations of kids have experienced
but it was rare for me
growing up in an Italian-American family
in the raucous
borough of the Bronx

Our lady

The feast day of Our Lady of Mt. Carmel is in late July, near my birthday. Grandma Sara liked to attend Mass that day at a church near Arthur Ave, the bustling, noisy epicenter of Italian food in the Bronx. People drive from Westchester and New Jersey to have a meal and/or take home treats from Borgatti's Ravioli, Casa Della Mozzarella and Madonia Bros. Bakery. After Mass, we went to Dominick's, a favorite, not crowded on a week-day. I had a pain in my lower abdomen so I asked Mom to come to the bathroom with me. I had gotten my first period. I was almost 11. When we returned to the table, Mom whispered I was a woman to Grandma, Aunt Ruth and Joyce, who hugged me. Then they toasted.

My dad and the nun

In 7th grade, Sister Edward hated me.

I finally broke a rule,
picking up a classmate's fallen shoe
during a fire drill.

Incensed, the nun demanded to see my parents.

They came in. She described the incident.
My father said, *Chris was only acting like a human being.*
Irregardless, said the nun.

My father knew *irregardless* was not a word.
He was silent.

For the rest of the year, any time there was
a discussion of school, my father would say,
Oh, you mean Sister Irregardless.

Pride

As I was growing up,
I became aware I was a good writer.
At 10 and 12, I won city-wide essay prizes.
But Mom, you and Dad—
urged me to be modest.
It was confusing.
It felt like a way to keep me down.
As a woman.
In my place.
I rebelled in high school.
More in college.
There I wrote a column for the newspaper.
I made radio documentaries.
I studied film.
I met a man who believed in me and my writing.

When I was forty, I went to an expensive shrink
for depression.
By then, I was a creative director.
She asked, *Did your parents ever tell you they were proud?*
That simple question lifted my depression.
Nowadays, we tell our son, we're proud he works for justice.
I tell my sharp, funny daughter-in-law, I'm proud
how she balances career and motherhood.
Even my little granddaughter, I told her I was proud
when she conquered her fear of water and
dog-paddled across the pool.

Because I've come to see that false modesty
is as terrible as dishonesty.

II

Not a fairy tale

In this story,
my father's an Italian-American prince.
My mother, a princess.
Both used to getting their way.
They appear happy for the first 10 years
of marriage. Not sure what happened then.
I began to witness loud, nasty fights.
The first time my father hit my mother
I was 13.
An only child,
I tried making peace.
No sooner would I make a deal with one,
the other would break it.
During these years, my Mom and I
talked often, over cups of tea.
I urged her to go
back to work, leave my father.
She always just shook her head.
As I started college,
she gave me a gift:
Concentrate on your career
she said.

St. Raymond's Academy for Girls

Parkchester, 1960s

For me, high school meant more nuns.
More uniforms—this time, navy blazers and
plaid pleated skirts. Ug-ly.
I lunched with Italian-American girlfriends.
After school, I hung with the bright, rebellious
girls who ran the newspaper, the debate society.
With them, I felt invincible.
Even though the most daring thing we did
was defy the nuns.
We had the Beatles, Joan Baez, Bob Dylan.
All of it, protest music, to my ears.
Along the way, I had my first boyfriend,
a year older than me.
When he went away to college,
he confessed he still asked his mother
to write his book reports.

Walks around the block
with Grandpa C.

Joseph Citarella

Beginning in my early teens
Grandpa and I started a summer routine
after dinner. We called them
walks around the block.

They gave me a chance to learn my family history:
How did you meet grandma?
Were you always a butcher?
The answers at the beginning were mostly
light-hearted stories of life, courtship, marriage
in turn-of-the-century New York.

Gradually, my questions went deeper:
Why did you leave Italy? How old were you?
Then I heard a dark tale of agrarian Italy:
my great-grandfather, a tenant farmer,
had been killed by a flying rock while tilling a field.
Grandpa became an orphan at 13.

Sometimes, a simple question got a complex answer.
Have you ever gone back to Italy? Yes. It seemed
Grandpa's older brother Vincent had forgotten
his wife and child back in Caserta.
So their married sister scraped together money
to send Vincent and Grandpa back to get them.

Grandpa's philosophy through life remained,
Sure, why not?

Fruit

Did I ever tell you
how much Italians love fruit?
Ripe summer peaches that
Grandpa liked to slice up,
dip in red wine
and pass to us kids.
Crisp apples that we got
when we came home from school,
the kind that crunch when you bite into them
and leave your chin all sticky-wet.
Pears so perfect my grown son still remembers
they came in brown paper bags whenever
my parents visited.
It's true we rarely had ice cream or even
packaged cakes. But
would you really miss them
when you had
a dish of cherries?

Squirrels vs. fruit trees

Grandpa really hated squirrels,
the way they killed the robins and
ruined the pears on his trees.
That's why he sometimes took out his BB gun.
It was really old—from the time
he and Grandma had the Highland Falls farm.
Of course, the gun was illegal.
The other grown-ups didn't approve.
But when they weren't around,
he'd try to frighten the squirrels away,
into the neighbor's yard,
the one who never said hello anyway.

Dandelion wine

Who would believe that
Grandpa made dandelion wine?
I admit it does sound fanciful.
But there I was, 13 years-old,
reading a novel in the shady backyard
on a hot summer afternoon.
Grandpa came out of the house
carrying a bottle with pale gold liquid
and two small sherry glasses.
He put his index finger over his lips and said,
Don't tell anyone. I only made
a few bottles of dandelion wine.
Perfect for a summer afternoon.

Aunts

Sometimes, on a Sunday afternoon,
I'd overhear my Mom
and her sisters' conversations.
Often they were envious
of other women:
Did you see her new outfit?
I heard they're going to Europe again!
Some people have all the luck!
And I thought
what a recipe for misery!
I had met many of the women
and they didn't look as stylish
as my Mom and my aunts.

At that point, I'd get up and find
my Dad, Uncle Lou, Grandpa.
And suggest a restorative game
of good-natured *briscola*.

Uncles

When Mary Trump wrote about
the sleazy comments
her Uncle Donald made about her teen figure,
I wasn't surprised.

I had my own creepy uncles.

Uncle Phil drank too much—
and looked lasciviously
at other women.

Uncle Ralph belonged to the *Playboy Club*
and thought he was Hugh Hefner.
He turned comments like
Looking good, Chris!
into leers.

Then there was Uncle Marco.
A strange man, quiet and stingy.
I rarely saw him smile or crack a joke.

I'd look at my aunts—
a beloved kindergarten teacher,
a tailor, a secretary—
and wonder what they had ever
seen in these men.

Playing with sharks

I learned to swim, play basketball,
even golf, from my Dad.
Patient and encouraging,
with him you played for fun.

But I learned to play pool
from my older cousin's boyfriend.
With him, you made the shots or
you left the game.
Hit the ball right here, firmly,
then pull the pool stick back
so this ball doesn't follow the first one
into the pocket.
Work the geometry!
I was 14. I hadn't studied geometry.

This ruthless instruction served me well
twenty years later at an advertising Christmas party.
I was paired with the head client playing pool.
Don't miss this shot, Chris!
Or what? I wanted to drive the pool stick
into his eye.
I made my shots. He scratched.
It should have ended the game.
It's a do-over, right? He appealed to
his sub-ordinate.
Sure, Geoff, he said. *It's a do-over.*

After the holidays, Geoff disappeared.
Word of the famous pool game
had reached his bosses.

The disastrous date at the Bronx Zoo

You know I used to love the Bronx Zoo.
So when John invited me to go there,
I was over the moon.
I'd had a crush on him for a few years.
He was tall, blond, easy to talk to.
I was 17. He was 22.
It was a sunny, not-too-hot June day.
We strolled hand-in-hand, rode the monorail,
watched the seals cavorting in their pool.

Toward late afternoon, we stopped to rest on a bench
under a big shady tree.
We were talking about fun things to do in the summer
—the beach, parks, miniature golf.
Then he asked, without preamble,
what I thought of the Church's position on birth control.
I was speechless.
At the time I thought he's scaring me off.
Now I know he was cutting to the chase.

III

Love and Politics

I came of age
in the late 1960's
so I ruled out boyfriends
based on their politics:
the cute ROTC cadet or
the clean-cut conservative.
But the sexy ex-Marine—
I did date him for a while.
He was the son of my mother's best friend.
I was fond of his family.
But I had to end it.
No matter how good
the sex might have been,
he wanted a wife and
a life in the suburbs.

I wanted to be a writer.

Thomas More College, Fordham University

Rose Hill campus in the North Bronx

It was still the Bronx
but a world away.
A 90-acre campus. Tree-lined walkways.
Gothic buildings.
Amid the tumult of the late 1960s—
civil rights, women's rights, the Vietnam War.
I loved the diversity of students—
friends who happened to be tri-lingual or bi-racial.
Female profs, passionate about their subjects.
Our feminist dean.
After 12 years of single-sex education,
it was fun to share some classes with the guys
from Fordham College.
I spent half my time at the college newspaper,
The Ram.
When I wrote an exposé on a lecherous administrator,
it almost got the paper shut down.
After that, I had a column with my byline.

Around that time, I became friends
with a tall, curly-haired guy,
one of *The Ram's* editors who covered politics—
the first anti-War marches on Washington,
all the campus protests against Army and
Dow (napalm) recruiting.
I took part in those.
We fell in love
it was wonderful
but Vietnam—and the draft—
didn't go away.
Still, there were concerts—
Simon and Garfunkel, The Mommas and the Papas,
The Chambers Brothers *The Time Has Come Today,*
booming loudly, urgently into the night.

My Dad and the Vietnam War

By 1965,
my Dad, a senior physical therapist
at the Bronx Veterans' Hospital
began to see a wave of badly injured
soldiers returning from the Vietnam
peace-keeping mission.
Paraplegics, amputees and
those with a new disease:
drug addiction.
The reaction from him, his chief and
all the Veterans' Hospitals was the same:
calls on Washington to send more
nurses, doctors, therapists, social workers.

Few came.

Instead, from 1965 to 69,
the number of patients rose dramatically.
My father's thoughts went from,
*we've got to win this so they won't have
suffered in vain to
we've got to end this and save lives.*

My dad's closest friends,
all physical therapists and
World War II vets,
changed their thinking, too.
I'd overhear snippets of their talks
at backyard barbecues.

By 1969,
the only people I knew
who still believed in the war
were my uncles,
none of whom had ever held a rifle,
thrown a grenade,
or been in a battle.

First dance

On that crowded dance floor
with live music playing and
strobe lights syncopating
we slow-danced to *Something*.
You didn't pull me close though
your hand was firmly on my back.
Still I found myself laying
my head on your shoulder.
It felt so natural even though
I'd never done it before.
I remember your soft rust-colored
sweater, your substantial shoulder
and the easy way we fit together.
I wasn't falling in love
just enjoying the feel-goodness
of the moment
when the music
and the lights
and the swaying of our bodies
all meshed together.

Our story

Writing brought us together.
That humor column I did for the college paper,
wondering what our ivory tower education
had to do with real life.
And your news story,
covering the first anti-Vietnam War March
on Washington, that was not televised.
We complimented each other's work
on the way out of class.
Wonderful column. Too good for The Ram!
Great story and photos. Felt like I was there.

Soon we were going to rock concerts,
foreign films, Alvin Ailey dance.

You didn't want to own me. Just love me.
How could I not
just love you back?

Being in Love in the Bronx Botanical Garden

Fordham University has a very pretty North Bronx campus.
But in the spring, for real beauty, you could cross the road
to the Bronx Botanical Gardens.
I don't remember fences or admission fees.
But then, we might have been oblivious.
Brian would soon have an off-campus apartment.
Yet, for the moment, on that perfect warm afternoon,
there were the trees, the lawns, the flowers in bloom
in that idyllic garden.

Advice

My cousin Sara and I
were sitting together,
the way we often did,
discussing boyfriends.
I was almost 21.
Sara was 2 years older
and engaged to Seb.
I told her Brian had asked me
to marry him. I had said yes
but it was a little scary.
She said,
But you love him, don't you?
You might not meet a guy
you love as much for another…
seven years.

Decades later
my daughter-in-law
tells me a similar story
about my son pursuing her in graduate school.
I had decided I wasn't getting married.
Then I met Emmet.
He was so serious about a future together.
It was a little scary.
I told my best friend and she said,
'Being a little scared isn't a good reason
not to do something'.

You're invited to celebrate the wedding of Christine and Brian

Saturday, September 12th at 1:30 pm
Fordham University Chapel, Rose Hill campus
(Map of campus and parking lot enclosed.)

Look for the small Gothic-styled church.
Don't expect *Here Comes the Bride*. The bride hates it.
Instead the organist will play the Beatles.
And *Handel's Hallelujah Chorus*.

Feel free to take pictures as Chris and her father
walk down the aisle. They'll be smiling.
And will probably look your way.

The reception will be lively with a great band.
Don't worry if your partner can't make it.
There'll be plenty of group dancing—
rock, the Twist, even the Tarantella.

There'll be an open bar, prime ribs
and strawberry shortcake.
Kindly RSVP by August 30th.

Before the South Bronx Burned

in the late 1970s

It's easy to mistake
familiarity for safety.
That's how the rapist
surprised me—
jumping in the elevator
at the last second.
He smiled to disarm me.
Then he showed me the knife.

I'm always cool in crises.
I fall apart later.

The good news:
The cops caught him.
Roe v Wade was law.
I could have gotten pregnant.
I didn't.

I'm always cool in crises.
I fall apart later.

Forty years now:
I give my last penny
to Planned Parenthood.
I pray for more tele-medicine,
abortion by mail.

All those women
cool in crises
can fall apart later.

IV

Escape from my Bronx

From the clutches
of macaroni culture:
petulant princes,
hair-trigger tempers,
'O Sole Mio.

From under the Church's thumb:
Mary or Magdalene,
goldfish glory or
martyrdom.

From the microscopic ear
and X-ray touch.

To the bigger pond
to unquestioning arms.

To the wrong friends
and the right mates —
all escapees too
from their Bronxes.

The Godfather Mystique

I've had colleagues confess to
loving those movies.
Wished they were Italian.
Like we're all *mafiosi*.

But those movies gave me
nightmares.
I'd wake up in a sweat,
dreaming I was married to Sonny,
the hothead, the killer.

In bed beside me,
my loving husband didn't get it.
But you're married to me
he'd say reasonably.

Lust

Over the course of a lifetime,
a long marriage
or relationship,
you'll meet men
who desire you.
And you'll have to decide
if it's worth it.
They'll be colleagues,
or worse yet, bosses.
Power as aphrodisiac.
Some will be the partners
of best friends or even
relatives.

I've never been good
at dishonesty.
I've had other priorities:
a husband, a son, a career.
No time to fit a lover in.
And maybe I knew,
instinctively,
it's not as easy as it looks.

Peace-keeping

It was a role I fell into
and then I embraced it.
When you have warring, operatic parents,
it's hard to look away.
Even on Sundays,
I was a peacemaker
between my cousins.
Often, I'd bring board games—
Careers, Scrabble, Monopoly—
to keep things congenial.

Years later, as a creative director,
angry or stressed account people
flocked to my office.
Life and death? No, only advertising.
I found if I just listened,
a lot of problems went away.

Now my peace-keeping's
on a small scale
with my grandchildren.
The little one, 2-years old,
wants everything his big sister has—
her toys, her shoes, even her dresses.
Sometimes she's fine with sharing.
Other times I need to intervene and
tell Kieran: *It's not ok to sit on someone
to get your way.*

I'm reminded of escorting
my 80-year old parents to doctors' offices
how they acted
just like noisy 2-year olds.

The Difficulty of Being Your Daughter

I know you loved me   imperfectly

Your expectations   were so meager

College   marriage   family

It would have never been   enough.

In that fishbowl of our family

I wanted   an ocean.

All those years   I was a creative director   I won awards

Did you tell your friends?   were you proud?

All those dinners   Easter, Thanksgiving, Christmas

Were they delicious?   or just your due?

You wanted   a nurse   a driver   a secretary

You asked too little   and too much.

Those last years   I almost threw in the towel

All those doctor visits   phone calls   and complaints

But I couldn't   I loved both of you   imperfectly too

Baking with Mom

I'd rush home from school
on those December afternoons
eager to start baking
Christmas cookies with Mom.

One day, we'd devote to butter cookies
shaped like Christmas trees and
candy canes.

Another we'd bake Mom's famous *Snowballs*.
We'd roll the dough the size of marbles because
the cookies would *grow in the oven.*
After baking, while they were still hot,
we'd toss them into bags of confectioner's sugar.

Even when Mom was in her eighties,
Joyce and I would trek over to her apartment
to bake with her.
By then she was *advising*
interjecting the conversation with reminders
Who's watching the clock? Don't let them burn!
Lower the temp of the oven!

I haven't been able to bake them
since she died.
But some December
when the grandkids are older
I'll head up to Albany and
show them how to make marbles
into *Snowballs*.

Matrilinear

My cousin Joyce was worried about her granddaughter, Sam, 13, who had fainted twice. The doctor took tests, but Sam was fine. *Did she have her period when she fainted?* I asked. *Yes, she had.* I remembered a hot summer day when I was 13, had my period, and fainted in church. My dad picked me up, carried me outside to get some air. I remember sitting on a bench, putting my head between my knees. Then I was okay. I told Joyce this story. She told Sam's parents. Sam fainted a few more times on hot summer days and then she outgrew it.

Campania on my mind

When I think of Campania
I see my grandfather's stories—
amid olive trees, tomato plants,
rows of grape vines.
Feudal land where the padroni ruled
so you were a share-cropper,
a tenant farmer.
I think of freak accidents—
farming and riding—
that killed two great-grandfathers.
I think how the North over-taxed and
tariffed you for more than a century,
made you feel
less
while they prospered.
How they drove you,
my beloved ancestors,
to come this far
to America.

Epilogue

What's our inheritance
from our ancestors?
If we're fortunate,
a good brain, fine looks,
a good heart.

I got my Grandma Sara's pluck.
In the 1920s, she and Grandpa
left 116th Street
to give their children a better life
in the North Bronx.

Fifty years later,
I fled the confines
of a too-traditional family
to find my place in Manhattan
as a career woman,
a writer.

My husband, a journalist,
shared the same dream.
We wanted to be part
of the bigger world.

When our son was six,
we sent him to the United Nations School
where we became friends
with parents from all nations.
He became a global citizen.

###

Now I'm about the same age
as my Grandpa was
when we began our walks

around the block and
I learned my family's history.

I try to be a grandparent
like Grandma Sara,
who knew just what I wanted
even before I did.
So far—with my daughter's hints—
I'm doing pretty well.

Every day I walk
over to the East River and
watch it flowing
north past Harlem.
I think of my cousin Joyce,
and my son Emmet,
the other nature-lovers
who live on the Hudson.

I feel the flow of family history
from Italy to New York.
From Harlem to the North Bronx.
My move to Manhattan.
My son and daughter-in-law to Albany.

And so the family flows forward
enriched with stories and recipes,
and these poems, that I hope,
make posterity proud.

Acknowledgments

The Truth about Skating won Honorable Mention for the Allen Ginsberg Award and appeared in the Paterson Literary Review.

Not a fairy tale and *My father's war* appeared in VIA: Voices in Italian-Americana.

66

The Bronx Years is filled with *vitalità*, writes poet Nathalie Handal, long-time resident of Rome.

It's the first poetry collection of **Christine Baldino O'Hanlon**. Christine recalls her rebellion, growing up in a traditional Italian-American family in the Bronx. Her poems examine her relatives with humor and honesty—and ask, what do we choose to inherit?

The centerpiece poem, *The Truth about Skating*, won Honorable Mention for the Allen Ginsberg Award. Her work appears in *The Paterson Literary Review, Voices in Italian Americana, Ovunque Siamo,* and in the anthology, *Rumors, Secrets & Lies*.

Christine has also written advertising—print ads and tv commercials—for cookie mixes, credit cards and US Postage Stamps.

www.ingramcontent.com/pod-product-compliance
Lightning Source LLC
Chambersburg PA
CBHW031126160426
43192CB00008B/1125